Duetcetera

Duetcetera

Ira Lightman

Shearsman Books

Exeter

First published in the United Kingdom in 2008 by
Shearsman Books Ltd
58 Velwell Road
Exeter EX4 4LD

First Edition

ISBN 978-1-84861-011-8

Acknowledgements
Some of the poems in this volume previously appeared in *Dusie* and *Arras*.
Duetcetera is part of a larger project titled *Coinsides*.

Duetcetera

UP the heat
to produce
forged splash
mettling film
that's a hit
for eyes sorely
to skim off
so cast your
charisma as well
already a stream
from old man
river for the
good of the
scenario spoiling
not by your
absence that
it would not
other than as
a poor real
-isation make
it in the record
except as diversion
to anything more
than what if
the scenario
that never was
a hit got
(re) made later
in the edit for
doctors of
historians of
philosophy who'd
multiply the
nurses of
values added

IF it bites
by contrast
of intensity
of air
to the hard
needed there
surface will
dawn waking
it as it
might go
to birth of
imbalancing
original
for lovemaking
destiny
made it so
sadly captain
of industrial
-ism would material
it so you'll put
however you
merely desire
on your prow
I ask you
so far ruined
in completion
of a sure dam
by drill & fill
insincerity as if
sincerity capped
your candour
found when we
enlarged
examination
to root and mine.

PAD approach unto
biographology ward
becoming that warm
ablebodied relative
portraiture locale
because 1 desires
lapdog contentment
homeworking all
parcel components
in an individual
by facsimile
from penhumanship
loners wherewithal
communally hated
runs the canvassing
for bubblinesses
of temperament
alternatives too
allegorically glossed
laminate covered
with hair loosening
cracked preservative
walls simultaneously
synchronous calms
and alternating
attention central
to accomplishment

SAUVIGNON levered arch
tablature cabinetted
filing habituate to
digitally recorded
screaming primally
to regress inside
prewar modernised
sinfully lacking
congregationally by
ritual mobile library
resembling unborn
generation of
contemporary friend
like John
"see me once
and see
the way
I feel"
singing rendered
over deed
thirty years ago
making parents
to be
for me
with you
in two
headed heart.

LAZENBY'S rigged   FIN-de-siècle-oke
ohms   redo
power acronyms's   realism soap
bond   that
with the secret   sweating profusely
rots   free
out in a field   of eavesdropped
"69"   glue
effort impacting   no. strengthened
love   on 1
reciprocated for   capitalizulated
unit   aged
kingdom's sticky   full employment
with   idea
head of the church   beyond trust
whom   body
carpentry grants   divided midway
buds   open
to woodwork past   again and again
pope   to a
carolling before   room of its own
vows   zest
for suitor would   gathering hours
tell   when
all but unto   the one goal
foes   jail
put upon knee   to the limit
that   with
sirs to primate   suspended parole
turn   like
vice v. never   knotted nooses
into   tied
padding for the   uniform for a
plot   laid
for interpretation   government class.

NO appreciation (as
depreciated stock
remakes) if not of
heartless film for
well-acted/shot odes

WE are all
no more than
puppets unless we
private affairs of
bel ami.

BEAUTIFY puns' dirt's unithorn   SAY of J's
drawn with a rose of presses   hey or blue
along with a wound's absented   way farther
success — waste and spot   sun inverted

sin, replant the waste   of groups
so a crater of soft clay   mysterious
double-exposes by slipperiness   in gospel
that'll kiss on film the day   Paul's new

the camera caresses? The film   TLMD® makes
is of camerawork, the dream   would be TRH©
of rotation slow to uphold   by jokes at
a volcano, shimmering   own expense

in rotation — red and gold   bodying whose
unnamed in the sight   flank & footnoted
sung music: music   4-square
writing words, words the   edging out

word — word the word-word   rivals who
rotating my head   sing
a-spin, my chest a-flutter   of offspring
in the throat on your lips   J's longings.

WHO let the dogs out
woof woof woof
who let the dogs out
woof woof woof
who let the dogs out
woof woof woof

like you mam
let the cat out
and I haven't
stopped all journey

CHILDHOOD of a form
noses to school when
repetitious adolescents
on cusp of tongue so
les petits pas sans
petits pas sonnez

decimating working
out your own way
consubstantiating often
one marking other.

OVERCOME
the rock of
beachcombing
your reach. I'm
carried dust
and lead us
to illness'
comeback as
a jackass
flat sick
at Gatwick

ONE recommends
awe and
sleep, finds
astoundingly
friend
shipped under
mind
beyond
in and
behind
England.

SHE seemed to say I CHRISTINE, I am in analysis
excitedly find you my recall as a humming
fellow with her eye forming on the motival

even in a pained chat. Bach planned business.
It made her dramatic Bach thus becoming
as a bull's tea-set. Bach markets economy.

NET accent
the formulae's
correct cases
fielding otherwise
no balls
and bowl
or catch
stroked more
than once
on a
side dishing
individuals exclusively
in play
thereafter's banked
stacked in
real boxes
over earth's
red core
whereat which
flicks first
like lighter
flame when
teams rarely
represented as
company dancing
truly herdy
then some
in extending
& contracting
wait room
time reading
books mid
conversation around
so gathering
fringes for
knitting pattern

PLAYING plays
play playing
played by
cocks who've
not fulfilled
chicks cooked
when sunny
grown up
we've been
late night
vegetarians to
the last
for good
the exception
being made
as love
babies from
time unprotected
we seek
as inspiration
fronts' rainy
climbing peak
pedalling cycles
the quiverload
in tongues
in wishes
fluttering over
the generations
whether we
for propriety
of thrown
voiced live
a topic
in our
passing of
anniversary presents.

WHAT may	THIS be
jan say	it now
but march	shall calm
august up	standing in
an aisle	john's withdrawal
one year	that overdid
by installments	the model
whacked landing	revolutions of
boys' blows	produced work
unfolded for	that direct
red girl's	business where
raspberry crush	we know
over snowy	days when
visually pleasing	splashes colden
unpragmatic type	to shape
set pavement	kick in
some eating	for both
chips off	of them
under fog	winning many
prisms broadcast	for God's
with spectrumally	made good
marginal pink	suddenly only
as white	on the
light box	make made.

REPUBLICAN   DEMOCRAT
unloved   the   unhated
hate   love
precipitating world's   cruising
the   within
anchor   ending   dry
yank   dock.

MOBILE		STATIC
moving image	file	stationary
elastically sighs		current crashes
to ripple on thigh	to	recede on front of
Sam Taylor Wood's		Stanley Spencer & wife
moving	anchor	caught
superficial		epiphanous
dancing	in	coasting
of Lord of		supper for
such fun	splintered	suffering
with boring men		unyielding who
statuesque	surface	painting gilds
& waving closes		lily to gasps.

LA recherche DE temps perdu
parmi les amis fait le demi-autre,
n'est pas l'hiver et
l'automne et l'été et
les printemps moins quart
du ciel des douze fils
sans père et mère,
néanmoins comme on dit en angleterre
fond présent.

WITH a crow   DARK queens
of cyborgia   your subject's
remote ain't   like the cat
by the mouse   fly-by-eye
plucked badly   a lyre sings
you ancient   that mice clunk
so bows judder   to fail avenues.

BE	THE
wife	life
governed	slovenly
by	my
lapses	perhaps is
it early	literally
aches	makes
a free	happy
hand	and
enough	bluff.

LOVE in a cold
climate o all
blue if a warm
January 5 next
morn as a dawn
icerink I walk
cool in a slow
measure I will
step as I know
symbols o love
take on a peak
passion I salt

SNAPPED a town
shut of a late
evening I find
best on a week
emptied o work
will to a calm
seizure o good
take be a film
Chaplin I know
copy as I film
century a warp
cuts on a weft.

UNO	LID 1 hundred & 23 millionth
dos	er with 4 hundred & 56 thousandth
tres	passes + 7 hundred & 89
quieren saber	teeth of them locking on
el	bow-out-of-the-way's
tren	cheatery
de	fending for what's marched on:
sus	hi we say, sulking little homers or not
letras	et al (ways, together) means
así	nine digits rub raw a plum thru wrapping.

STARE
spirit in anger,
not daring
unfairly
cruel ripostes
to breathe
from your mouth
spelling a rebuke
in minor crystals

THE conceited
of poet lives
just spelling
stroking into pages
like doodles
becoming two
in dimension
inside a composition
as about developed originals

TREE
of God
flow charts
in workbook's
1-2-3 sums
and dying
to be pruned
flattening molecule
thin as plug's prong.

PERHAPS prayer is   KIDS' lie troo
in the deregulated   upon pooh song
when sense experiences   olé
high capitalism   old grew
and becomes senselessly   grey old cod bod and
sensually   supped pursed
sense making   lips kiss but
not I who took the   cut
money, who took the money all   the
ways, to a stop changing   tie singtone
fits out wards   ringtime terse
with a regionwide pass   verse said sage paid page
shabby but readable   rage
that doctors   scope score ay
(ay!) contact   by concert
out of the contract   concept
getting on   gall hall
to progress   nearly measly quasi
stab don't dial   stash
hole in its   fast east
bodies   german herman
substituting mnemonics'   wall
mnemonic with 3 letters   walk to
separate to digit   um sick pick
phoned betty boop to   nix
hearing   mix crick brick
aid   thru tipt water
CALL to ONO or   waves have hate
NOM to   quit suit
666   nam mam man
used to getting onto   neuro metro
that you   mood nome spoof
want   prone
a gulp of   proof past part
insomniac's dreamcup   anti knuckles around.

I WOULD not   UPGRADE
lay so bloody   justly
print on it;   public works
excerpt, without pressure   justly
yet my cell   print on it;
being the travelling   public works
while I'd work   justly
what's on knee   public works
of me there   being the travelling
here, not aside   excerpt, without pressure
with an 8   upgrade
leg drive squiddity,   justly
yesterday's healing tentacle   yet my cell
cut must breathe   lay so bloody
only so it   with an 8
knits today's mouth   justly
as I score   public works
worksheet with unsplitting   molecule-combining like christmas
press called more   in the love
than given occasion   sighless, my bus
molecule-combining like christmas   of an unconvinced
paper suppleness my cadence,   I miniheaved
deserted limited openplan   public works
company born anew   justly
in the love   public works
of an unconvinced   upgrade
post Nuremburg subordinate   thus sheetworking that
brigging never you   upgrade
thus sheetworking that   public works
cadence, I miniheaved   justly
sighless, my bus   public works
eavesdropper changing seat   justly.

YOU, evasive   AS some fear
romeo, stunned   spring singing
me as stags give earholes clear
& leave wound   with advancing
graffiti & bound to be duetting.

SACRAPPARENT!   ACQUAINTED my
what was that   related via a
means to land   married above
slid families   frowning once
under a happy   one had so by
deal or soles   work of a DNA
& court cards   that unseeing
as that would   at all copies
low muttering   far theatrics
counted games   through trees
by totallings   like a Coptic
& transparent   helichopper's
non-secondary   environmental
adolescent as   for the radio
swaddled upon   quasiwaveform
primary gangs   and biography
fed man after   tolls in life
comprehensive   at least thus.

THAT DEVICE'S edifice
i.e. edified art
blocks fallen together
raw as shacked chantier
in town be holding
recorded reading
of foreign language
tinkle for accompanist
undissonant
with trick in establishment
not there as biographer
hereafter the crown
notwithstanding the same
as a pro-game
at cards, one triangle
untwins without collapse

I WANT to know
how somebody is
feeling their way
for the harmonies that's
the readthrough as
familiar property
we may option as
lead is gold music
to the box
office in heroic
role keeping life
of his teeth in
cross fire tapeloop
of curb eaten
by lily . . . livers like
whole framed for them.

CURIOUS	CIRCULAR chain lettered
prostitute	hole that encumbers
genealogizing	collars then whirring
absent	necklaces dialling numbers
characters	getting through
within	as who
the	impatient stationed
visitors	at the end of their tether
book	so from tomb & with whom
at	will they go together
partying	getting through
all	as who
related	present future past
can	eye use to cast
never	dye in the colourless face
make	redder arterial
hugs	of mystic material
by	blushing on the better embrace
tree	of the saviour of behaviour
renewborn	when I've deadwood to say
absorbing	I already making steadily
only	nonsense man anyway
absently	getting through
centres	as who.

I FEED you habitually   FOR YOU crave all I
although my child   habituate in the past
of neither the adverb   successfully, only as I
yet or the you are known   to do it have never

you, I feed all so   habituated ever
me fed of toast buttered   until then & the feint
from the uncovered dish   signal is to cry out not
for me, the fridge for you   when I shovel

and I part hungry at   your banquet of minibite,
time, so at the double   your slice to my slice of
(you copy) fast which grown up in   a sandwich of wolfing
ghosts in safer butter   for fridged butter scarcer.

B (ye) man&wife   "¡AY! & 1 4 nun +
(of) love (free)   nun 4 1." Any1
by (my) gap (per   <musket> ears
haps is) it early   any0 shot: what
(lately) aches   1 looks @, % ages
(that made) free   with traduction's
(me) hand holding   (powered) books
(&) enow (bluff)   flatter, € por £.

NEVER LATE's one's late   4 + 20 blackbirds
& all said & done   convected in a storm
eternity returning me   sung a song of sixpence,
who ended young   a pocketful of form

in office has timing   when the storm would open
to wait or make 'em wait   the birds beginning singing
if mirroring's loving   wasn't that so daintily dished
love's enigma we hate   to set before the king.

CAN IT, in a tick,
you!
You've got a minute
to honour the chickenleg's
wee swing
proofing napkin
in little crescents,
to recognize a degree
is Bigendian country
redrawing for war
overlaps
at the making shore
of gest you're
as telling
to a child whom
neither cat nor scrumper
of own bubble poaching
curiosity doesn't kill
forever,
for forever
tatter-tethers the whiter
egged on by hot yolk

A MOMENT, please
Mister!
Autumn there mid-fall
dropping by due date of
ripened
platter down lumbered chutes
X m/s to Y s/m
I batter
around only fishneck
stockinged in toy plastic
at the crease
of the century
mid-millennia for
nothing
fizzes in a column
foretold yet now here
by your side of
passover ribs
show time
considerable less considering
than Solomon's finery
fluttering the bookish memories.

REMEMBER the led better
life
next
to the good
accommodating
situated
comic
less the brief
scripted and more the
character if you buy
enough to keep a
float in the black and
am I or have I ever
improvised
into the repertory
din of tuned prudes
a scene of acts,
a bar of movements
affording a stage
in development
of stars to twilit
junior saxophone
and synthesiser concert
trilling the modern instrumental
commercial break sponsored
politicians' meeting on stuck
cadence or noise
at distorting levels
until we come
to be fed back

DON'T know why with
inspired
steps
tiptoeing the cartoon
clown
vehicular
transport
tickles in rigidly
adult viewing frame of
reference no longer for
many who grown up
colourless half the time thus
been tortured by dizzy pacifiers
post-war
of the boom
engineering signposted shortcuts to
remapping body politic
in flick book form
as I rub
your genii up
burp channels, verbing the
metaphor alive
I see at playback
storytime speed lifts
move on spot
opening to new outside
like teleporting in
momentarily throws if
unremembered to compare as
held mine presto yours.

MERELY abominable TVs
within the mouth
watering next Ulysses
2ft from my trousers
so opportune a star
acrorhymes 4 x r

EVERYTHING I'm
pokering in time
although by hatred
& bulimia of stress
I can't call in id
eality the less.

AN 1882 metal snake's
historic city is coming to yes
section by section come
in with such attack in time
o lock in not forever
composite erring spur

GIVING birth without
the womb considered
as a process but
only the product
creates the doubt
in matter of fact.

COOL credit   MANGY meat
couriers cooking   muddle mouth
career cure   mastication mired
cultivating   masking mash
coaguacultural   mid myth
country cuisines   man made
creeded composters   mislaying mother.

A WORK colleague
has a nephew
younger than me
or my son who's
walking earlier that
is than mine not yet
but what stands by to
shading this account
split from all infinitive
grammar of rhythm
as part rugby
and part soccer
cross bar
shall show
without
net
it now
catches
deadening the shot
to arrive still
glued to
spot

BY MY family
in my father
or my mother
inlaw ground
is to falter
as we vigils
await change
of my method
to be unique
alive dancer
as so nearby
to my family
angry proofs
go to widows
or to absent
comes report
if he walked
or he lacked
earth family
by it by one
member blink
early yonder.

I WROTE that I	DIDN'T, no, why, well
herein thing	what I tell
through beads	I tell only that poet
I took in sights as	critic, forgot
way to master	else in reply
stand — still	like gull whose style
sound like sweat	impression I'd flappily discourse
suddenly starker when nothing	on he'd discuss
going to go on as before	not, it was that thus
around the cross firing	and my Perseus
of a lot of bull	memory sees this
up to	hover the eyes
in air	talking Muldoon over gravy
guitar everywhere	in the pub mirror with Davie
musakking the transaction	when it seemed on the poetaster's puns
of birth, fate & friendship	I talked mine to come, when utilitarians
to bear	lose the response rhymes
dispersed psalmody	and antiphony Bethlehems
when God will	fix as Brit heritage and accent
speak to the reassembled	majority constituency government
not unalong puritan lines	out of historical passion orbits
that pound the fabric	in space on holes once in time planets
of our red carpet when	you have gay unfriendly parishes
beyond it at universatility that shall	polarize genii wishes
certainly hurt	still only a non-sinner
don't mince what	knows the last dinner
of meat there is	of idiom,
to spare	as we cross space / time
living in families	as we might have ours bid grace
that gamble	just only in case
like shepherds fanning banked notes	the fumbling way should be meant's
in the last chance bar	resemblance in epochs' establishments.

ARK com DOT gibbous looking
plaints strange masters without growing
unto, from rise anointed took in
commitments doublepaged centripetal to show
staunch coupled fielder of vision,
hence all'd stand then to bow(l)
over sold life of mission
stylish, stalled viceroy in lieu,
be in to reckon punctuated
news your ways that is halo
whiskery mandarin hallowed when peels ring
said poor weds old, and slow
appetisingly concentrated preverential vernacular generation,
postskimmed breastmilky, postfigures plucking a new
Barnstaple circulated, literature notes' period, un
irks illk ited antique through
stimulating, necessarily historicals as we imagine
weepy, cloud moods in situ
that pity like ours, palely being
reveilled shortloud bedridden by stirrups like buckets.

PAPARAZZI WERE THE verifiers' baby by
f-stop a charge with meaning
the Benjamin in the running
a Dickensian slap bang out
of the Bible of youth into
shaken by fullness our
grip that daddy the dolly
catches the shot mummy
without the stall or circle
outside at seat snugged spy
forge after pre-crawl hope so
first firing style is sin
thus beyond to be fami
shed tinkering liar blamed, de
lighted moving also strapped for
authority on phraseology or quote
me so we're no less
on that stuck couched in
Cobainistic armchair and suite
I rejig apart or grouped
barnacles to edit in
billing Europe to style humility
he'll not pay at its peril
for intended of artless dodgefulness
otherwise advances Welsh for bannsaid.

YOU AND ME's us if we DEAR, we
mayn't show us disgraced graces
thus yet then won't lightly disestablishing
seen us being us upstand
fired at night where river mouths
anew bank managed account
on surer to Eden's
throat preferably trading
unchattery from route
draught cashewing advantaging
almost all in to tongue of
discomforted uncontrol UKcraniuming to
which won't slip thin
let out nevertheless running
the 2 nights lordly
stay till repair worded
due, then beneath to make
renewed hell, image's plinth mistress of masterful
laid on to historically
contracept heating Tudor-beamed
by residue retouched out of need
like cooling draft for sermon
being half falls to the hawks
of ashen bun fingers downsized.

MORTALITY sees only
its one solstice
so in a mortal
lifespan's precise autumn's

central heating
at the centre
feinted
the Indian Summer home as

henceforth constant
"on the safe side"
in the room
substituting precise equinox

now in suspension
for benched swivel
of Institutions Inc a
maker of the machine

the institution buys
changing against the haze
slow shaking
head of an automatic

cone to "Here Comes the Sun"
turned out throughout where
go in
the unrealised that

half-appeared
describing a soufflé
as a baby breathes
staple sleep, duck the origami

tree decoration
Christmas breezes.
December always lifted bills
to release about the spring

YOUR LONG body had a heavy head,
so half-teenager in walk
ambitiously measured
but on swaying stalk

like a sunflower of six feet
you moved, vulnerably
entering church to meet
our gathered assembly

lively at the last
then drunk at its reception,
with a dashing past
of faraway gentlemen

somewhere implied in eyes
twinkling at our camera.
You would surprise
yourself, none other

than tall thinking John,
equally stunned by CD
systems, travels on
earth, history

and erotic prints
you'd hand across in
opened book. Hints
that we miss it begin

that haunt of life
and detail of days,
the later strife
to making memories

of good company.
You loved life's feast
and impressed on many
how it's seized.

I DON'T know, me.
Lover, am I dejected in this
goring? Struck, yes. I fear He
in my assailant wounded & is
hers and mine to pine? Bliss is His

[St John of the Cross]

It shows me you've gone somewhere,
sweetness, that I'm dejected like this,
gored. Were you, are you not there
in the square holes crossword fillers miss
to parse us the tense of bliss?

[St John of the Cross]

```
I insist    IT'll B
O missed    ever O
U exist    asked Y.
```

STRAINED beneath
bellow prayer,
mouth there
upon body
low lip
in an
I O
is to
lap the
feet that
hands raise
tuning ladder
towards extreme

NOTE tearfully,
gather oneself
as a squeezebox
where blushes
gape as we fold
out to Christ,
who's that
alert to our evil
ministerial
wash of hued
cleansing, whether once black hard leathery
to white page He conjures our spacetime
like a kerchief through His hand.

THERE'S NEVER to the there-ever
which we imagine there-after
another physicality like a farmstead to
occupy, sewing to the weather
a-long. A-strong business
instead, to become dwelling
proportioned to the swelling
greeting not dawn. Tenderness
dethroned its advance
of ordered worldly
hairline, otherworldly
and mechanical wordbarns
stored unrepeatably
yarn teased by combs into treaty

THE MEMORIES of you
and I find you
round you, round me
as an arm-army
wee-strongarms withal
you be, keeping small
my response: to
ensconcing you
held my-head-high
mirrored (my-my)
like a memory
to miss in me the
you being made till
is parent-mortal.

SHOULD IT be ONE MIGHT abide
by unfailing shore tide
dry land would leave silent
submerged, shush pent
into something — fascination,
one study in concentration,
deupholstering the curveball
over our heads — so cluster blind's pupil
focussed each fragment come
up scratched in one's time
current bubbled allowed
part to swallower & swallowed
shoal, closet-cell-combed, fleet
now hypocrites to the fat
as if post-corporation
all in trance nation!

COATS my body   NO SWEAT by contrast the wax
dying   of white lilies' to yours. Smell
underground   these new have attracts
a church's stake   away from yours who'd cobble,

atop the let die   who's at layering of my boot
and caped caniner   that scarce had as much leather
filed away me,   when bought; you'd thwart
dehallowing exflowery me 4 my itchies craved air. A

style going plain   ceaseless strike of hammer as you
to taste of   nail mockingly
rival bloods   underside in, to
nearing overall   transfix a queer, wanderlust, envy

the homely es of the   will magic slipper – o foot
ich nearing uberich   fittingly or castrated?

[Mallarmé]

IF U have no time 4 imitation
of the jist's
righting right & left
also you're in the thread

YOU can't pluck azure
lavender to try ingratiating
mascara wink sure
for a sale, I'm not decorating

who need to burrow
for you are you alone
screwed off for mean . . .
jist . . . sloughs

bare walls with mats
in my room in absolute room
for one's belly rat-a-tat-tats,
won't settle for a blue fortune

or promethean booty necked
with U? Right not 2 B netted
sometimes in the edification
of breath if great power left

when it's best nestled in floppy
bob of hair. You'd put
reek of poppy
fields, ma petite,

but weed getting Bethlehem
ticked off, petal, by portal

bring home chez maison
creepy crawlies of the season.

[Mallarmé]

GASP crashes in   LIKE clockwork, for an editor
station, hang laid   and never the number
on us — humpin'   4 hangover, this chirpy sewer
safe save the maid   'll always hawk the first #.

[Mallarmé]

PROLIFIC read he   ALSO smoothing patio round
is political not   a neat plot that'll ping
in platters, everly   probingly, a poet's bound
spins on spot   2 2 B at its daily unearthing.

[Mallarmé]

COLLOQUIALLY aramaic GUILT to unpaid courtesy call's
scannable phoneme less once breath's garlicky
parties' line to break on you, dewy about it all,
fidelity (could be) to blaspheme with addition of onions, quickly.

[Mallarmé]

SHE SHOULD allegory   HOW
synonym at him,   can I be bad,
he allegory   when
metaphor from her;   she
should her re-allegory   says
synonym from him   some
re-allegory   thing
metaphor at her   good?

[Robbie Rotten]

THESIS & antithesis ballroom
dance round one's bagged
if it gets the hand
or lose the valuables
weighing up not even a saw
before
the first time you read Proust
or last
whereafter you live him
in the mind involuntary
th(r)ough echoing ways there
as U borrow not much from Rome
but infra
dig dresses of twin
habitually differently voluntarily
recalled at the expense of
information through
it though
the cells of a
conscientious
object
for all to conscript
to war not body
among men
would kid
itself

IN HISTORY of song and
discs back to their place
some are 45 or 33
exclusively, or ultimately
a 78 min CD plays with itself
other CDs in a changer
smoothly and we lengthen
on the spot
spinning a general seizure
across hemispheres wide webbing
felt in establishment starting
to suppressurize the tide
red as a tonic
clonic clenches of the fist
an air sphincter eyeballing
floppy thus winks
saluting like a wave
weak within
a sea of fire
and inhibitedly
oriented
for now where thoughts
going with sun
at the worms
underneath
flat earths unrim.

INSIDE creaking like that through wonky ships
is close home's webbed out not that
outside drifting wall's float opened for scuttle
does that like by in every searching
interrupt by life the time corner for
corrupt rapture will space that of a
rapt behind in time still circle
secret a yield field

SLOWLY go below the elbow,
darling mine,
let's be sled beyond the tents and
rugged
contention
rucked
around the urgent. Tents of tents
by mealy might shall be peaking,
may congregations butterfly
pillar slapped
hungry as paper
ministers: how to collide, scope
serial-primarily

I GIVE in, can't you
sense tonight
the treasure's aura, you toss up
air
coins
when
you've wont to scent, not pounce
hands squander-floundering, fish
netting blanket ahoy,
spearfree riverboy
whoosh flurries
minute whorls, stretching to be known,
pegged.

MEMORY motherlode mistress of all mistresses   FRAY
o you sum-it-up of pleasure o you sum-it-up of hard work   frat
stand in the mind for the beauty of all caresses   feat
the soft pile hearth the je ne etc quoi of eve   neat
s memory motherlode mistresses' mistress   nest
evenings bathed in crackling firelight   best
and evenings on the balcony everywhere pink fog   bent
you and your soft breasts tender heart   pent
you and i speak together in the undying ways   pant
evenings bathed in crackling firelight   part
the sunset of those evenings' beautiful warmth   dart
their spaced-out depth their muscly heart   dare
tending towards you queen i adore   care
in my deep breaths i felt i scented your blood   cape
the sunset of those evenings' beautiful warmth   jape
the night suddenly solid as a courtyard   jade
and my eyes in the dark on a quest for yours   jape
and i'm inhaling you o softness o drug   cape
your feet slumbering in my brotherly hand   care
the night suddenly solid as a courtyard   dare
it's the cushy number to evoke the happy hour   dart
and go back to a past sat on your lap   part
yet is it tenderness to be on the hunt for beauty   pant
and not lead myself to you your body and soft heart   pent
it's the cushy number to evoke the happy hour   bent
shall our commitments our scents our endless kisses   best
be reborn from old wells we're forbidden to plumb   nest
as a newly teenage sun clambering into the sky   neat
having come washed from the deepest horizon's ocean   feat
o commitments o scents o endless kisses   frat.

[Baudelaire]

STRANGE he island in faith. Music to   LOOK right
like New tanned sand with the film,   and left
with an inevitability   after it that
Margaret exceeds the   strafed

mindedness. Picard?   off! Stay drawn:
is a noble a family?   to flanks
pose offer   of a basin,
its complex   wet banks
human power in dance shares   to void
feeling the dance needed   plinth-plateau,

Darwin. Greek – what   alloyed
you for the Star Trek   bowl

atonalism. Given hi   of your own
shock, the blackly   cell-reproving
picking up kit to   stone
Karen Black   life   unanimity, unmoving.

[Rilke]

EYES front personnel
because fight geometer
slotting in other
drones if you fail
to equal parallel
and plus perpendicular
once Lokavibhaga curves number
Rome sowed hierarchical
flatlining metronome
of lines consigns,
to future of form,
number in the tock
of a clock
of arrest's V of ones

UNDER sunset bluff
shrifts gigolo wrong
like bloody rough
lives gleaming along
beginnings to begin
empty of our shit
notwithstanding sin.
I: "that's it!"
Spirit's betrayal
crucifies my chest
and dreamy funeral
puts that to rest
in a string vest
safe as Noah's girl.

[Baudelaire]

SHOULD BUS pass & U don't fight
for its might other's dawnings
known added value of nothing
sitting on the board
planked on clefs boxed in perspex
scraping you noble
lord of the sky
being almost summed in chords
that long to reign over
Northumbria then Bayreuth
returning too repressive upon one
benefit arpeggiated from love

THUS tautening my back I see
worrying colleagues hurrying me
for something to say
while I ate to please
some work to come
to the pieman who judges
crust thin and holding
on to be carried
shoulderheight singing
dispersing the bounce
even to a riposte it's
exactly how I felt this might be being.

MOBILE in the
trouser pocket
windowside on my leg —
a husband's in an aisle seat —
sang the scale of its recharge.
I to a diarist dizzily
linked — almost through you
123 texting on that free hand
held, by the zoomed-by
sill mine's
plugged into

ONE MEMBER of
my team found
the robot whose base's at these
coins' beck. Fitting the batteried
Volta inventor's xmascounterdemand,
including the furrow left to up
of my eyebrow, not on his conscience —
so seamstressed companionship
following a stomp in
the
renaissance.

THIRTEEN by three   HOW   THE EVE includes
is a measure   so   you turning round
of workable wood   ever,   about the weekend
that without ordering   and   changing a generation
showed up today;   to   object by subjecting
call it 39   where   you have tolled
not, make wide   so   like a bellow
and long equations   ever   the volcanic decade's
red come, carpentry   else   casts sonnily accerebral
bulging past geometry   your   air of placed
on rough not   belonging,   scopes watching under
graph paper, crafted   my   blackcatwalk to mark
for discipliny letters reciprocating sparky's animus damp.

ANYTIME IT'S personal in the
sense of undertouching person
snap-corrosively picking on guts
once my twin soul,
publication, title
sees these alternate embedding
fractioned with a mission
and the other fractioned on board
tight more in and then on end
of time honouring of
liking bit somewhere where taster
at the fountain
by copycat
expected rulebinding
extended from the pap
isms cheesy as choice more sold
to those own no baedecker recipe
finally melting into a spirit guide

SPRING out of orthodoxy's
rushing bum to salute a hymn
to undoing reflex tap dance's
degenuflectedly erect
at premiere
as if with any promotion might
equal with one's supper
at communion very swiftly
it, be, understood standing by self
preserving leaves home
that has not been dismissed driven
to plume outed
history forgiveneverly
as for you
create in dynasty spiralling
on dynasty working street of local
down maided tinned ale evenings
stain-spectrum panes skin handled.

YOUR reporter once whistling   POST by the forests, fingering tree
of the harps his pout-song   glissandi'd as zephyr, leaves blind
yelling "timber" to disarm groups   down on fish tin piano templates
(some response to Bach's bequest!)   & turn now to the uncivil
high on neck-brassy arsenal's latest   trump & party on them, the first
settler of the tale's new and interim   world's symphonic theme.

[Virgil]   [Virgil]

THE DEATH FEELING for kids
who see their folks argue, or who
become aware the
slow change yuck of folks stuck in
how what makes us vulnerable

when we share with our partner
& they see us hardens into
crabbiness lest they say, yup, I
don't really like you, I can't allow
U to be U at any point at which

that makes it hard for
me to be me,
because that's where the bonding
goes in our foursome,
total waste of an hour

and feelings
of hitting the wrong note
instead of the right one
and these are the petty incidents
that push every couple to ask,

if only in bleak rage that passes
for the point? It's the fate of a child
and there is almost no
relationship they can be born into
that doesn't face deadness

in the married. Yet
as a tutor friend of mine said,
never forget I
teach lots of kids with rich parents,
given lots of time, and still

I rarely met the like. The same
is true of your two,
I say just feel our feelings.
I'm reborn, mustn't make arrivals,
in rage or in ectasies of art, hide

I THINK
there are
forces of
conservatism,
and they are entrenched,

but I stop short at an Icke style
"10ft lizards rule the world"
approach;
it seems to me
it's the playground,

no-one understands
why we all act
on these common-sense
generally held bullyings,
and knee-jerkings,

that get circulated,
I put it down to sin,
to Satan,
but not to one party or group;
clearly, the Republican-leaners

in business and the media
didn't know who to replace
"w" with
whom they anyway didn't want;
that's always been my take,

that Blair looked and thought,
madman at the helm. Forces
don't hold the reins,
who can't get their man elected,
and still are curious

about the candidates
thrown up by democratic process.
The enemy's cynicism, from which
can you or I say we fully depart or
which of us shall scape whipping?

I VERY much like
playing and
I don't have
a small dog Patch, with a wet
snuffly
nose, and
I don't throw sticks
and play with him. So
it's nice to play with friends

I LOVE counterpoint, in
music. Two (or more)
voices weaving together
one a slow and other
skittering about
going up the scale
simultaneously down
sometimes coming together
to make harmony a moment.

I QUITE like
baby brother Quentin. Daddy took
us to a place once in the car
where we met a
poet-man who liked to peck
Quenty on the head
(with a wallop of his face)
the way a woodpecker pecks a tree
if it did it in a few big pecks.
The poet-man raised Quenty above
and he lowered down his head
like a football player for England
doing a goal
with his head
then shoved his face
quickly
but nicely
at him,
as if to say Boo with it,
but he said Knock
and Quenty laughed
and laughed
as the man did
it all again, and kept
doing it
making Quenty laugh

SINCE my mid-twenties
a contrapuntal
poet which would have suited
me more than conceptual
poet, the name I made
of myself not knowing Kenny
Goldsmith's use of it,
lurked in me, after
NYC, before PR.
John Ashbery
double-columned in Litany —
which I tried to perform
with a friend
in a cabaret once
not in a
contrapuntal musical way,
certainly not following
classical counterpoint,
dropping in
Cage (collecting for a circus)
crackle echoes
and weaves human voices
but it is not
trying to create the
feeling of
collido-colluding on a harmony.

MUMMY AND Daddy
were dressed up nice,
to meet the poet-man.
The poet-man
was from America,
Daddy
had really wanted to see him,
Daddy likes
to take us too to places.
We did get lost
in the car. Daddy said,
at one point,
"that's not right"
and then he looked for
a roundabout and
a quiet road
and stopped the car.
He checked the map, said,
"yes, ah, right, Daddy gets it,
Daddy's clever enough
to sort this one out",
and he did say
while we were getting there,
"late, late, we're going to be late"
and then we got there,
in a sort of village

FOR IF Ashbery
has a greater confidence
I have less in the voice.
I lessfluence
compared to his
finesse with words,
a
pausing
I do not do so....
.... Ashberically
wryly
over a bon mot,
a well-phrased turn
being
more gawky, so I have often gone
for a tone
I press on with puns.
Geoffrey Hill calls them
howlers, phrases resonant if
with potential
to be read awry
when I see the work
in print, that is, though
they may be vulnerable risks,
whose afflatus is deflated
by him before you.

WHEN WE were there,
Daddy saying
yes, that must be
them, and I think
I know her
parked the car,
looking at a group
of people in the small
scrub backyard
where we only
just fitted
in, by driving
backwards and
forwards short
amounts a lot, and
Daddy turning the steering
wheel and looking in his
side mirrors a lot.
There weren't a lot of cars.

POETRY forms
talk to me, too,
forms that make me feel
don't back down
from my feeling even if I
express
vulnerability
and, more curiously,
forms that prod,
encourage me to be
more
explicit, feelingful,
daring
in nimble
contracting
groups of words to one
impacted neologism
I did not dare to know.
I knew to dare.

THEN DADDY was really
pleased to see the poet-man
and dashed up
very quickly, excited
and gave him a handshake
and a hug, and asked him
about travelling from America and
I heard Daddy ask
the poet-man if we
could all see him do his poems,
and were they
"suitable for children"
and the poet-man said
very warmly
but in a grown-up way,
Definitely No.
Mrs Pubbus
used to tell me which poems
she thought were good or bad
and sometimes too grown-up,
I thought
she really
feared
poems
she did and did not
talk
about badly read outloud

IN MY band,
we didn't attempt much
call-and-answer lyric writing,
though
there
was that relationship
between music and voice.
McCartney
said it's getting better
all the time
Lennon was all
with melodic counterweight
it couldn't get
much worse. We
wrote for and to each other,
I'd offer something for
the other to hear,
not deflate, but
trouble
to come up with an exploitative
counterpoint
had the potential to feel
good art in the draft
technically, with double
probe, even
use
Escher scales upon B&W.

THE PLACE wasn't a museum,
not white, not
big rooms. It was a bit
like the B&B where
I got salmonella i.e.
dusty
and dark without much
light in at the windows,
like having
curtains
pulled across. And the poet-man
and Daddy
and some other people
were going to do poetry
in all the rooms.
Somebody was asking
everyone doing poems
to pick which room
and which bit of a room,
to do their poems in
which worries Daddy,
deciding things,
and thinks he takes
a long time. I like
deciding things, and I
don't like hurrying. He
did decide a room. It
had a big protruding table
in it, and he put his
laptop down on it, and
looked for plug
sockets, walked
up and down a bit

AND I want
to add
when I make translations
notes I cut and cut from the first
draft. I go into very very
free paraphrase,
then lose 90 percent
and leave
10 percent as a nuance. I want
to add a footnote about this. Two
columns leave me
the chance to do a sidenote,
as long as all
sidenotes
I believe "go a bit Dada."
Dadaism generated
by chance and process
tam-tams the canon
with its chutzpah
etc. I'm
enchanted by
metaphoricity
(now there's
a long word) it's
how I myself
am metaphor. Similétude
burns no bulb, mouths a keystone
for scream swell
of all the like
out
to tail (living the)
night's groggy horse
day(dream)ily rocked.

THE poet-man
said to me, "I told my
oldest boy, he
had to put up
with the baby
for one year. But
at the end of that year,
if he wanted, we
could send the baby back
so shall we . . ."
This is playing.
But I have to be sure
we're being fair,
in our hearts, and
no-one's being nasty,
in their hearts. So
I said a very
big fists-up NO!
CAN'T TAKE
QUENTY. But I wasn't
cross. I was just
being play-fierce

I WANT to keep
writing the way I talk to
purposes. I
paste long wound
concoctions of words,
which is what
the ear looks to find when
sing sing
singing
into verse and chorus.
This is phrase for rarefied word.
Gertrude Stein only learnt
a few words at school but
Carl Sandburg is a child distrusting
fancy words when you're grown-up
but less homely fair and meek and
Buckminster Fuller
was giving one
work to
file as much as Renaissance
translators throw away translations
like newspaper 4 unclown thought.

DADDY WENT off
and we stayed
in another building
just over
from where
the car was parked.
A lady
was there who was
making herself up
a lot. She said
she really liked Frankenstein,
and I told her
I really like Dr Who,
and by the way
I'm a vegetarian.
And she said
how old are you,
and I said six
and she said, well,
I'm a vegetarian
too. And I
said what are
you doing and why
are you
painting
your face green
and she said, I'm
painting myself
green to look
more like Frankenstein, see
this is my
Frankenstein
suit. Because I like
Frankenstein, and I
always have

BUT I wasn't writing
like that, until
I got married: I was
writing very very Dada,
very esoteric, very over-written,
I married the need to be direct.
I needed, not the double-column form,
but to look at, maybe, how 2 strains,
mine, plus my new wife's,
were producing a child, both of us,
the best of both of us,
and something else
nuggety growing out of us. I was also
trying to be a vicar.
And had a new family of in laws.
I wanted to be a vicar and
that's what,
opened my new family, and many
new people,
in my giddy state of love to me. They
looked at
me as
simultaneously
doing
something detached from them,
on their behalf,
struggling to put something
ideal into words. I felt
like writing
some plain and
heartfelt lyrics, but,
once written, they
looked gawky on the page. I
tried putting them aside to
side, literally.

DADDY asked
if anyone would like
to do any
of his poems with him?
There were just enough
people now
to fill
the room,
standing around
the oval table,
Daddy with the laptop on.
Daddy held up
a painting
he'd brought and did
funny
voices
holding it in front of his head.
He played
songs that he sang
like a tongue-twister
trying to read all the poetry
on his laptop screen, and the
screen was full
of words, to the
tune of a
song he likes playing
on his ukulele, and doing
it all in
quite a loud voice

SUSPICIOUS
flat earth terminology
commands, as
Buckminster Fuller says, I resist.
I try to understand
to the point
of neighbourliness
there is no
up and down in
universe.
Rather, the in
and off
of pilots
saying "I'm coming in to
land", and "take off"
and this is true generally, so that's
Buckminster Fuller.
Fuller's
nice to use terminology
as it occurs
is sometimes with and without
under
but
not past
being mucked about. Plus
I believe in a transcendent future
from unwobblingly pivoted
the present as
of Pound translating Confucius.

AND when
he stopped that,
I said
I'll do it with you,
Daddy, even though
I never had, and he
let me. I'm
getting good
at reading, and I
read some
of the words
on his laptop screen
and he
read some others, and
a computer voice
on the laptop
was saying words too

ANYONE else felt
there is
child-like language,
also beginner's guide to grammar
language, in modern poets
like
Rob (in Sentences) or Lyn (in
My Life) or Carla (especially
in In The Mode Of), or Leslie's
early work with its feel of
lullaby and nonsense poetry
quote unquote, or
Bruce's Wobbling
or Bernadette's Studying
Hunger; can this be just
put down to the spirit of play
or camp?

DADDY finished, and
people clapped us. I
heard a lot of people
say to Daddy, That kid's
so great! You
want him to be
like that
forever. If he
grows up and
stays like that, he'll
be doing well. Daddy
told me
later
again how they'd
said those things, and
he said
lots of times
to Mummy
and to me
how happy he was
with what I did. And
with no practice, and
no rehearsal, he said

IT SEEMS TO me
to be a vital distinction
between
some Language Writing and,
on the one hand, fifties and sixties
Concrete Poetry, on the other
hand, the always urbane JA. That
there is a kind of defiant,
politicised, fascinating
use of child-like language, that only
a forceful radical
group could do, to make
potentially hostile readers
frightened of it, so that it doesn't
just get dismissed as childish as
don't children also get dismissed
as childish when
they want to include something
normally excluded? Isn't
Carla Harryman's work
in particular
interested in using Langpo"idiom"
to open up this very area?

THEN WE left. It
was getting dark, at
the end of the day.
Daddy drove
us a little way to
another town, and we
stopped at a chip shop. I
met a really nice
little boy and we ran
around for a bit, with
Daddy telling me quite
firmly but not really
crossly to make sure I
looked out for cars, as there
were lots of parking
spaces in a car park in
front of the chip shop.
I had a pineapple ring,
and chips, and Mummy
always really likes curry,
and shared chips
with Quenty. I get to sit
in the front of the car
at least until Quenty
is one, maybe longer,
while Mummy sits
with him in the back
to feed him
and talk to him
and tell him songs.
I nodded off a bit
on the way home, and
Daddy put me to bed with
no time for bath, with a story

WAS there
an opium den,
Mrs Pubbus?
I home in on
one year,
under her rage
now gone, she who
said to be
toughing it
said
not not
not not
what she said
let alone what
she meant. I pace
the playground
Monday,
Tuesday,
Wednesday,
Thursday,
Friday
horribly moved, static
from my own
child's and my own
rage. To trust
a teacher for our children
we have seen grow
and sit at their parties
not feeling their cries
I cannot abide. It is opium.
I rejoice the year
is done. The child
knowledge accounts
veils of smoke screen rent.

INDEX OF FIRST LINES

Lightning Source UK Ltd.
Milton Keynes UK
21 August 2009

142946UK00002B/42/P